ML

11/93

THE KNOPF POETRY SERIES

ALSO BY EDWARD HIRSCH

For the Sleepwalkers

This is a Borzoi Book
published in New York by Alfred A. Knopf, Inc.

Wild Gratitude

Wild Gratitude

poems by

EDWARD HIRSCH

Alfred A. Knopf New York 1986

821
H61W
1985

THIS IS A BORZOI BOOK*

PUBLISHED BY ALFRED A. KNOPF, INC.

Copyright © *1981, 1982, 1983, 1984, 1985 by Edward Hirsch*

All rights reserved under International and Pan-American Copyright Conventions.

Published in the United States by Alfred A. Knopf, Inc., New York, and

simultaneously in Canada by Random House of Canada Limited, Toronto.

Distributed by Random House, Inc., New York.

Owing to limitations of space, all acknowledgments for permission to reprint
previously published material can be found on page 79.

Library of Congress Cataloging in Publication Data
Hirsch, Edward.
Wild gratitude.
I. Title.
PS3558.I64W5   *1986   811'.54   85-40348*
ISBN 0-394-54848-5
ISBN 0-394-74153-6 *(pbk.)*

Manufactured in the United States of America

FIRST EDITION

For my parents, Irma and Kurt Hirsch,
and my sisters, Arlene and Nancy Hirsch—
and for Janet Landay

Contents

4

May I, composed like them

Of Eros and of dust,

Beleaguered by the same

Negation and despair,

Show an affirming flame.

—W. H. AUDEN

For all the insomniacs in the world
I want to build a new kind of machine
For flying out of the body at night.
This will win peace prizes, I know it,
But I can't do it myself; I'm exhausted,
I need help from the inventors.

I admit I'm desperate, I know
That the legs in my legs are trembling
And the skeleton wants out of my body
Because the night of the rock has fallen.
I want someone to lower a huge pulley
And hoist it back over the mountain

Because I can't do it alone. It is
So dark out here that I'm staggering
Down the street like a drunk or a cripple;
I'm almost a hunchback from trying to hold up
The sky by myself. The clouds are enormous
And I need strength from the weight lifters.

How many nights can I go on like this
Without a single light from the sky: no moon,
No stars, not even one dingy street lamp?
I want to hold a rummage sale for the clouds
And send up flashlights, matchbooks, kerosene,
And old lanterns. I need bright, fiery donations.

And how many nights can I go on walking
Through the garden like a ghost listening
To flowers gasping in the dirt—small mouths
Gulping for air like tiny black asthmatics
Fighting their bodies, eating the wind?
I need the green thumbs of a gardener.

And I need help from the judges. Tonight
I want to court-martial the dark faces
That flare up under the heavy grasses—
So many blank moons, so many dead mouths
Holding their breath in the shallow ground,
Almost breathing. I have no idea why

My own face is never among them, but
I want to stop blaming myself for this,
I want to hear the hard gavel in my chest
Pounding the verdict, "Not guilty as charged,"
But I can't do this alone, I need help
From the serious men in black robes.

And because I can't lift the enormous weight
Of this enormous night from my shoulders
I need help from the six pallbearers of sleep
Who rise out of the slow, vacant shadows
To hoist the body into an empty coffin.
I need their help to fly out of myself.

Fall, falling, fallen. That's the way the season
Changes its tense in the long-haired maples
That dot the road; the veiny hand-shaped leaves
Redden on their branches (in a fiery competition
With the final remaining cardinals) and then
Begin to sidle and float through the air, at last
Settling into colorful layers carpeting the ground.
At twilight the light, too, is layered in the trees
In a season of odd, dusky congruences—a scarlet tanager
And the odor of burning leaves, a golden retriever
Loping down the center of a wide street and the sun
Setting behind smoke-filled trees in the distance,
A gap opening up in the treetops and a bruised cloud
Blamelessly filling the space with purples. Everything
Changes and moves in the split second between summer's
Sprawling past and winter's hard revision, one moment
Pulling out of the station according to schedule,
Another moment arriving on the next platform. It
Happens almost like clockwork: the leaves drift away
From their branches and gather slowly at our feet,
Sliding over our ankles, and the season begins moving
Around us even as its colorful weather moves us,
Even as it pulls us into its dusty, twilit pockets.
And every year there is a brief, startling moment
When we pause in the middle of a long walk home and
Suddenly feel something invisible and weightless
Touching our shoulders, sweeping down from the air:
It is the autumn wind pressing against our bodies;
It is the changing light of fall falling on us.

Omen

I lie down on my side in the moist grass
And drift into a fitful half-sleep, listening
To the hushed sound of wind in the trees.

The moon comes out to stare—glassy, one-eyed—
But then turns away from the ground, smudged.
It's October, and the nights are getting cold:

The sky is tinged with purple, speckled red.
The clouds gather like an omen above the house
And I can't stop thinking about my closest friend

Suffering from cancer in a small, airless ward
In a hospital downtown. At 37 he looks
Boyish and hunted, fingered by illness, scared.

When I was a boy the summer nights were immense—
Clear as a country lake, pure, bottomless.
The stars were like giant kites, casting loose. . . .

The fall nights were different—schoolbound, close—
With too many stormy clouds, too many rules.
The rain was a hammer banging against the house,

Beating against my head. Sometimes I'd wake up
In the middle of a cruel dream, coughing
And lost, unable to breathe in my sleep.

My friend says the pain is like a mule
Kicking him in the chest, again and again,
Until nothing else but the pain seems real.

Tonight the wind whispers a secret to the trees,
Something stark and unsettling, something terrible
Since the yard begins to tremble, shedding leaves.

I know that my closest friend is going to die
And I can feel the dark sky tilting on one wing,
Shuddering with rain, coming down around me.

Fast Break

In Memory of Dennis Turner, 1946–1984

A hook shot kisses the rim and
hangs there, helplessly, but doesn't drop,

and for once our gangly starting center
boxes out his man and times his jump

perfectly, gathering the orange leather
from the air like a cherished possession

and spinning around to throw a strike
to the outlet who is already shoveling

an underhand pass toward the other guard
scissoring past a flat-footed defender

who looks stunned and nailed to the floor
in the wrong direction, trying to catch sight

of a high, gliding dribble and a man
letting the play develop in front of him

in slow motion, almost exactly
like a coach's drawing on the blackboard,

both forwards racing down the court
the way that forwards should, fanning out

and filling the lanes in tandem, moving
together as brothers passing the ball

between them without a dribble, without
a single bounce hitting the hardwood

until the guard finally lunges out
and commits to the wrong man

while the power-forward explodes past them
in a fury, taking the ball into the air

by himself now and laying it gently
against the glass for a lay-up,

but losing his balance in the process,
inexplicably falling, hitting the floor

with a wild, headlong motion
for the game he loved like a country

and swiveling back to see an orange blur
floating perfectly through the net.

The Emaciated Horse
Chinese painting of the Yüan Dynasty

It was as if I had stumbled alone
into another world, someone else's dream
    of floating jade mountains, a stone cliff
dropping to a moonlit blue lake
    surrounded by willows, one village
winking through the distant clouds,
    another puckering in the gray mist
like a paper orchid wrinkling in water.

It was as if I had somehow stumbled
into someone else's mind: in one painting
    I knelt beside a small, middle-aged
woman on a muddy riverbank,
    gossiping, wringing out laundry;
in another I stood on a steep ridge
    staring into the forehead of heaven,
shoulder to shoulder with the lightning.

I escaped from the celestial power
of that light and paused beside a young girl
    sponging her neck, two courtesans
powdering their shoulders with talc,
    kimonos gathered at their waists.
Their lips were the color of plums,
    their eyes were as shiny as porcelain.
I heard lightning exploding in the distance,

    a branch cracking somewhere in my mind, rain
and sleet washing across the tented willows.
    The wind gusted through the wet leaves.
And suddenly I found myself staring
    at the stark, inky gray profile
of an emaciated horse:
    gaunt and bony, half-starved, a shrunken
towering remnant of a once-splendid body,

that horse was someone I could know, someone
that I had already known for a long time.
          It was drawn on a faded handscroll
    by Kung K'ai, a familiar of emperors,
          "a strangely isolated man"
    who had become an *i-min*,
          a pariah, a late survivor—
like his horse—from an earlier dynasty.

    This was the same artist who had once drawn
large, fearsome creatures racing furiously
          through the countryside with their nostrils
    smoking and their warlike black eyes
          blazing in anger, their coarse manes
    flying in the mountain wind—
          and I kept trying to imagine him
kneeling on the dirt floor of a one-room house

          patiently spreading out a paper scroll
    on the back of his eldest son, carefully
          drawing the slow, torturous outline
    of a starving horse, a dying
          horse against a vacant background.
    One gray horse and nothing else.
          I had seen that stark creature before;
I recognized its harsh, inhuman profile.

    And then I was seven years old again.
I was in the city with my grandmother
          buying Christmas gifts for my parents
    and the emaciated horse—
          yoked tightly to a gilded carriage
    of wealthy, laughing tourists—
          was standing next to us on the crowded
street corner, waiting for a traffic light.

The city was wearing its brightest colors,
but all I could see was the woeful figure
of a horse, a gaunt survivor
from a previous dynasty,
waiting for the light to change,
for the tourists to dismount,
for the taxis to start moving again,
for the intolerable burden of its life to stop.

Edward Hopper and the House by the Railroad (1925)

Out here in the exact middle of the day,
This strange, gawky house has the expression
Of someone being stared at, someone holding
His breath underwater, hushed and expectant;

This house is ashamed of itself, ashamed
Of its fantastic mansard rooftop
And its pseudo-Gothic porch, ashamed
Of its shoulders and large, awkward hands.

But the man behind the easel is relentless;
He is as brutal as sunlight, and believes
The house must have done something horrible
To the people who once lived here

Because now it is so desperately empty,
It must have done something to the sky
Because the sky, too, is utterly vacant
And devoid of meaning. There are no

Trees or shrubs anywhere—the house
Must have done something against the earth.
All that is present is a single pair of tracks
Straightening into the distance. No trains pass.

Now the stranger returns to this place daily
Until the house begins to suspect
That the man, too, is desolate, desolate
And even ashamed. Soon the house starts

To stare frankly at the man. And somehow
The empty white canvas slowly takes on
The expression of someone who is unnerved,
Someone holding his breath underwater.

And then one day the man simply disappears.
He is a last afternoon shadow moving
Across the tracks, making its way
Through the vast, darkening fields.

This man will paint other abandoned mansions,
And faded cafeteria windows, and poorly lettered
Storefronts on the edges of small towns.
Always they will have this same expression,

The utterly naked look of someone
Being stared at, someone American and gawky,
Someone who is about to be left alone
Again, and can no longer stand it.

At this hour the soul floats weightlessly
through the city streets, speechless and invisible,
astonished by the smoky blend of grays and golds
seeping out of the air, the dark half-tones

of dusk already filling the cloudy sky
while the body sits listlessly by the window
sullen and heavy, too exhausted to move,
too weary to stand up or to lie down.

At this hour the soul is like a yellow wing
slipping through the treetops, a little ecstatic
cloud hovering over the sidewalks, calling out
to the approaching night, "Amaze me, amaze me,"

while the body sits glumly by the window
listening to the clear summons of the dead
transparent as glass, clairvoyant as crystal. . . .
Some nights it is almost ready to join them.

Oh, this is a strained, unlikely tethering,
a furious grafting of the quick and the slow:
when the soul flies up, the body sinks down
and all night—locked in the same cramped room—

they go on quarreling, stubbornly threatening
to leave each other, wordlessly filling the air
with the sound of a low internal burning.
How long can this bewildering marriage last?

At midnight the soul dreams of a small fire
of stars flaming on the other side of the sky,
but the body stares into an empty night sheen,
a hollow-eyed darkness. Poor luckless angels,
feverish old loves: don't separate yet.
Let what rises live with what descends.

Tonight when I knelt down next to our cat, Zooey,
And put my fingers into her clean cat's mouth,
And rubbed her swollen belly that will never know kittens,
And watched her wriggle onto her side, pawing the air,
And listened to her solemn little squeals of delight,
I was thinking about the poet, Christopher Smart,
Who wanted to kneel down and pray without ceasing
In every one of the splintered London streets,

And was locked away in the madhouse at St. Luke's
With his sad religious mania, and his wild gratitude,
And his grave prayers for the other lunatics,
And his great love for his speckled cat, Jeoffry.
All day today—August 13, 1983—I remembered how
Christopher Smart blessed this same day in August, 1759,
For its calm bravery and ordinary good conscience.

This was the day that he blessed the Postmaster General
"And all conveyancers of letters" for their warm humanity,
And the gardeners for their private benevolence
And intricate knowledge of the language of flowers,
And the milkmen for their universal human kindness.
This morning I understood that he loved to hear—
As I have heard—the soft clink of milk bottles
On the rickety stairs in the early morning,

And how terrible it must have seemed
When even this small pleasure was denied him.
But it wasn't until tonight when I knelt down
And slipped my hand into Zooey's waggling mouth
That I remembered how he'd called Jeoffry "the servant
Of the Living God duly and daily serving Him,"
And for the first time understood what it meant.
Because it wasn't until I saw my own cat

Whine and roll over on her fluffy back
That I realized how gratefully he had watched
Jeoffry fetch and carry his wooden cork
Across the grass in the wet garden, patiently
Jumping over a high stick, calmly sharpening
His claws on the woodpile, rubbing his nose
Against the nose of another cat, stretching, or
Slowly stalking his traditional enemy, the mouse,
A rodent, "a creature of great personal valour,"
And then dallying so much that his enemy escaped.

And only then did I understand
It is Jeoffry—and every creature like him—
Who can teach us how to praise—purring
In their own language,
Wreathing themselves in the living fire.

2

It must have been a night like this one,
Cool and transparent and somehow even-tempered,
Sitting on the friendly wooden porch of someone's
Summer house in mid-October in the country

That my father, home from the Korean War
And still in uniform, wearing a pilot's bars
And carrying a pilot's stark memories (still
Fingering a parachute in the back of his mind)

Jumped from the front steps where he'd been sitting
And held a sweating gin and tonic in the air
Like a newly won trophy, and flushed and smiled
Into the eyes of a strangely willing camera.

It must have been winning to see him again
Safely home at the close of a vague war
That was too far away to imagine clearly,
A little guarded and shy, but keenly present,

Tall and solid and actual as ever, and anyway
Smiling past the camera at his high-school sweetheart
(Now his wife, mother of his two small children)
Surrounded by friends on a calm midwestern night.

It must have been so soothing to have him back
That no one studied him closely, no one noticed
That there was something askew, something
Dark and puzzling in his eyes, something deeply

Reluctant staring into the narrow, clear-eyed
Lens of the camera. I've imagined it all—
And tonight, so many light years afterwards,
Looking intently at a torn photograph

Of that young soldier, my distant first father,
Home from a war that he never once mentioned,
I can foresee the long winter of arguments
Ahead, the hard seasons of their divorce,

The furious battles in court, and beyond that,
The unexpected fire, the successive bankruptcies,
The flight to California with a crisp new bankroll,
The move to Arizona with a brand-new family.

Tonight the past seems as sharp and inevitable
As the moment in Indian Summer when you glance up
From a photograph album and discover the fireflies
Pulsing in the woods in front of the house

And the stars blackening in a thicket of clouds. . . .
It must have been a night like this one
When my mother glanced over her husband's head
Into a cluster of trees emerging behind him

And heard the wind scraping against the branches
Like the *strop strop* of a razor on rawhide,
And saw the full moon rising between the clouds
And shattering into hundreds of glassy fragments.

Twelve years old and lovesick, bumbling
and terrified for the first time in my life,
but strangely hopeful, too, and stunned,
definitely stunned—I wanted to cry,
I almost started to sob when Chris Klein
actually touched me—oh God—below the belt
in the back row of the Skokie Theatre.
Our knees bumped helplessly, our mouths
were glued together like flypaper, our lips
were grinding in a hysterical grimace
while the most handsome man in the world
twitched his hips on the flickering screen
and the girls began to scream in the dark.
I didn't know one thing about the body yet,
about the deep foam filling my bones,
but I wanted to cry out in desolation
when she touched me again, when the lights
flooded on in the crowded theatre
and the other kids started to file
into the narrow aisles, into a lobby
of faded purple splendor, into the last
Saturday in August before she moved away.
I never wanted to move again, but suddenly
we were being lifted toward the sidewalk
in a crush of bodies, blinking, shy,
unprepared for the ringing familiar voices
and the harsh glare of sunlight, the brightness
of an afternoon that left us gripping
each other's hands, trembling and changed.

Now the city deepens in smoke,
now the darkness raises a withered hand
        and the night begins, like a prelude,
in real earnest. This is the music

        that hurries pedestrians home
and follows a fading breath of ashes
        out of the faded commuter stations.
Slowly the bridges open their arms

        over the river and the cars
fan out in the mist like a peacock's
        feathers, or a deck of luminous cards
dealt into shadows. This is the hour

        when the tugs slide into their cells
and the gates snap shut behind them, when
        prisoners stare at their blank ceilings
and windows are bolted in factories.

        Some of us remember the moon:
it is a tarnished silver ball worn
        into our memories, a faint smudge
of light rubbed into the heavy fog.

        In this city even the ginkgoes
turn up their collars in self-protection
        while the buildings stiffen like hills
against the wind. And as we hurry home

        in the cold, in our separate
bodies, it takes all our faith to believe
        these black drapes, this curtain of ash
will ever rise again in the morning.

It's that vague feeling of panic
That sweeps over you
Stepping out of the #7 train
At dusk, thinking, *This isn't me*
Crossing a platform with the other
Commuters in the worried half-light
Of evening, *that must be*

Someone else with a newspaper
Rolled tightly under his arm
Crossing the stiff, iron tracks
Behind the train, thinking, *This
Can't be me* stepping over the tracks
With the other commuters, slowly crossing
The parking lot at the deepest
Moment of the day, wishing

That I were someone else, wishing
I were anyone else but a man
Looking out at himself as if
From a great distance,
Turning the key in his car, starting
His car and swinging it out of the lot,

Watching himself grinding uphill
In a slow fog, climbing past the other
Cars parked on the side of the road,
The cars which seem ominously empty
And strange,
                    and suddenly thinking
With a new wave of nausea
This isn't me sitting in this car
Feeling as if I were about to drown

In the blue air, *that must be*
Someone else driving home to his
Wife and children on an ordinary day
Which ends, like other days,
With a man buckled into a steel box,
Steering himself home and trying
Not to panic

In the last moments of nightfall
When the trees and the red-brick houses
Seem to float under green water
And the streets fill up with sea lights.

The dead heat rises for weeks,
Unwanted, unasked for, but suddenly,
Like the answer to a question,
A real summer shower breaks loose
In the middle of August. So think
Of trumpets and cymbals, a young girl
In a sparkling tinsel suit leading
A parade down Fifth Avenue, all
The high school drummers in the city
Banging away at once. Think of
Bottles shattering against a warehouse,
Or a bowl of apricots spilling
From a tenth-floor window: the bright
Rat-a-tat-tat on the hot pavement,
The squeal of adults scurrying
For cover like happy children.
Down the bar, someone says it's like
The night she fell asleep standing
In the bathroom of a dank tavern
And woke up shivering in an orchard
Of lemon trees at dawn, surprised
By the sudden omnipotence of yellows.
Someone else says it's like spinning
A huge wheel and winning at roulette,
Or drawing four aces and thinking:
"It's true, it's finally happening."
Look, I'm not saying that the pretty
Girl in the fairy tale really does
Let down her golden hair for all
The poor kids in the neighborhood—
Though maybe she does. But still
I am saying that a simple cloud
Bursts over the city in mid-August
And suddenly, in your lifetime,
Everyone believes in his own luck.

Sleepwatch

In the middle of the middle of the night
            it is a dull tom-tom
    thudding in your chest, a ghostly drumroll
        of voices keening in the dark, words
vibrant with echoes, keeping you awake.

The body next to yours is already asleep.
            Already you've lost it
    to invisible caves, the slight stirring
        of leaves in a wet field, the crescent
of another man's face flaming in the trees.

Outside, the snow falls into yesterday's snow,
            tomorrow's stormy rain.
    But, inside, a moon shivers in the spaces
        between your wife's outstretched arms, between
her shoulders and her legs, between the skin

of water pulled over her watery lungs
            and the white egg growing
    larger and larger in her chest. This is
        the same moon that shudders in darkness
inside of darkness, behind your eyes.

Last night you walked along a cold, snowy beach
            and watched a flock of gulls
    flapping into a drift of stars, a drift
        of flakes thickening on the water
like a mist of empty hands. You paused,

but your dog loped hopelessly downbeach after
            them, swallowed up by fog,
    too far away to call. It was like this:
        your legs walked a stark beach, but your hands
were at home fastened to your wife's body.

All night you could feel them rising and falling
      on the dim waves, helpless
   in moonlight, wanting to be anchors, mouths,
     wanting to be anything else but hands
drifting farther and farther out of reach.

Tonight you're alive in your own dank forest.
      And now the body
   sleeping next to yours makes small gaping
     noises, like birds flying overhead
with an alien upwards gesture.

But down here all your bones make music.
      Down here in the middle
   of the middle of the night, you're awake
     listening to the steady drumroll of a heart
ghostly with losses, your tribal chant.

The Night Parade

Homage to Charles Ives

I

Officially, the parade begins at midnight
When the vice-president of sleep calls the assembly
To order while the sergeant-at-arms bangs
A drowsy gavel against the empty brown forehead
Of the podium and all the slumbering senators
Turn over at once, bleary-eyed, weary, and
Still a little drunk, though a few junior
Republicans from Idaho and Mississippi
Rise up in their plush seats to applaud
The honorable gentleman from Alabama calling
For a vote. The burly speaker announces
That the unanimous motion of sleep carries

And on the well-lit corners of Maple and Elm,
On Main Street in small towns and villages
All over America, the children of sleep stand
In plaid nightshirts, rubbing their eyes,
The veterans of sleep surround the flagpole
For that brave radiant moment when the first
Notes of the National Anthem of Night float
Over the bandshell like balloons and then
Drift across the bleachers of the high-school
Football stadium where the janitor and
The assistant principal are preparing to fire
A cannon and spangle the sky with stars.

And now the mayor of sleep shakes hands
With the owner of sleep and the newly elected
President of the Chamber of Commerce, and maybe
He even pecks his wife on her fat cheek.
This is the signal for the prom queen to hop
Into the back seat of a ghostly blue convertible
Driven by her blond boyfriend who is already
Dreaming of the moment when he can park
The triumphant car by the lagoon and slip

His arm around her naked white shoulders.
Because at night in even the smallest towns
Desire spreads through the body like a stain.

2

That's why his cousin with the thick glasses,
Braces and skinny blue legs is sobbing
Into her pillow, refusing to dry her eyes
Or comb her hair, refusing to listen
To her mother in pink curlers and a silky
Gray nightgown, even refusing to look up
At her beloved father in maroon pajamas.
Later, she will watch the night parade on
Television, like hotel clerks, night-watchmen,
Prison guards, waitresses in all-night diners,
And—like insomniacs all over the country—
She will stroke the cat and gulp warm milk.

But she won't see the new junior executive
In the established firm of Bradley & Bradley
Slipping from a motel room in Miami Beach
Registered in Mrs. Bradley's name; she won't
See the Young Democrats in massage parlors
Or the Communists and the born-again Christians
Handing out fervent leaflets to pedestrians
Who smile and nod; and she will never see
Naked men touching themselves in dark theaters,
Or whores adjusting their uniforms, or drunk
Conventioneers rubbing pink lipstick out of
Their white collars, muttering excuses.

The greatest moments of the night parade
Take place under the open tent where muscular
Sleepwalkers tiptoe across tightropes, carefully

Holding up umbrellas, and two married acrobats
Float through miles and miles of empty space
Just to hold hands on a wooden platform
Hammered into the air. Everyone laughs
When the clowns of sleep mimic the lions,
Tower over the midgets, and pinch the backsides
Of beautiful bareback riders. And everyone
Drifts home slowly when the half-moon dims
And confetti falls from the sky like applause.

3

The televisions are droning at the Hotel Insomnia
Where every room is identical and no one feels
Like seeing a parade on a black-and-white screen.
It's boredom that keeps the businessmen watching
A rerun of the seven o'clock evening news and
The housewives restlessly switching channels
Between a dull soap opera and a musical comedy
About a rich Italian who falls in love with a poor
Girl from southern Iowa. The movie finally ends
And everyone listens to "The Star-Spangled Banner,"
Waiting for the message of blankness that follows
The message of patriotism at the end of every day.

And so all the televisions whiten at dawn,
The radios blur with static. The stragglers
At the town hall and the junior-college gym
Pull down the last orange and black streamers
And snap off the skulls of the last beers
Buried in the cooler. Happy musicians, baton
Twirlers, professional pool players, and
Even the hit men for the syndicate of sleep
All clamp instruments into heavy black cases
While the sheriff leans back in his dark chair

And the sentry dozes off at his dark post
And the custodian of wind vanishes like smoke.

The cedars and pines stand in an ashen trance.
At this hour even the staunchest insomniac
Falls through a gaping hole opening up
In his body like a flower or a fresh grave.
And now the long arm of exhaustion reaches
Across the rooftops to douse the candles.
That's why no one ever sees the pale trains
Pulling out of subways and abandoned stations
All over the country; no one sees the ghostly
Trucks and gaunt steamers loaded with bodies;
No one sees the blind searchlights or hears
The foghorns bellowing in the early morning.

3

No one remembers him anymore, a boy
who carried his mattress through the town at dusk
searching for somewhere to sleep, a wild-eyed
relic of the Old World shrieking at a cow
in an open pasture, chattering with the sheep,
sitting alone on the front steps of the church,
gnawing gently at his wrist. He was tall
and ungainly, an awkward swimmer who could swim
the full length of the quarry in an afternoon,
swimming back on his back in the evening, though
he could also sit on the hillside for days
like a dim-witted pelican staring at the fish.
Now that he is little more than a vague memory,
a stock character in old stories, another bewildering
extravagance from the past—like a speckled seal
or an auk slaughtered off the North Atlantic rocks—
no one remembers the day that the village children
convinced him to climb down into an empty well
and then showered him for hours with rocks and mud,
or the night that a drunken soldier slit his tongue
into tiny shreds of cloth, darkened with blood.
He disappeared long ago, like the village itself,
but some mornings you can almost see him again
sleeping on a newspaper in the stairwell, rummaging
through a garbage can in the alley. And some nights
when you are restless and too nervous to sleep
you can almost catch a glimpse of him again
staring at you with glassy, uncomprehending eyes
from the ragged edges of an old photograph
of your grandfather, from the corner of a window
fogging up in the bathroom, from the wet mirror.

Fever

In Memory of Anna Ginsburg, 1893–1977

So the fever leans back in its icy chair
and lies to her about the night. She thinks the
full moon is German; she believes the empty white face
of the moon is saying that it wants to arrest her
for plotting crimes against the light.

And she can't sleep. It's as if the fever
had dropped a cube of dry ice into her throat and
it is scalding hot. No, it is the smell of gas seething
in her chest. And she keeps hearing footsteps,
the wind pronouncing names in the street.

She can't get up. She is so drugged
that she can't focus on the living room wall
or see the stark painting that hangs above her chair.
It is a picture of the sky above a stone house
that is crumbling in a stony field.

She can't forget the night the fever
interrogated her for hours. That was before
it flooded the country and left corpses in the trees,
bodies floating face-up in the muddy streams.
She can't forget their faces, either.

And she keeps hearing voices. Someone
says the night is like a sick child who raves
and cries out in her sleep because her head is on fire
and she sees the tall pines bursting into flame,
waterlogged corpses going up in smoke.

Sometimes she dreams about a red setter
barking furiously at a squirrel who is racing
across the branches for its life. Always she can smell
the singed brown fur and feel the thin squirrel
finally losing its balance and falling.

She whimpers. And that's when shadows
begin to grow out of the wet floor, the water
rises along the misty walls. The windows are barred
against the night, but the night waits calmly.
Muskrats paddle in a neighbor's yard.

And now she is drifting in a shadow
against the door; now she has fallen asleep
in her own chair. So the fever holds her in its arms
and all night she dreams about the dark clouds
and the white moon coming to arrest her.

Ancient Signs
In Memory of Oscar Ginsburg, 1894–1958

He loved statues with broken noses,
the flaking white bodies of birches
after disease had set in,
the memory of peasants
kneeling at garish, hand-carved altars.

He loved old women washing laundry
by the river, coolly slapping the
bedsheets senseless on the stones.
It was sixty years later
and yet he still couldn't forget them.

And he was still ashamed of the damp
bodies of men's shirts filling the wind,
flapping about like chickens
at the signs of hard weather.
Only a woman's hands could calm them.

My grandfather loved thunderstorms.
He loved to see the restless weaving
of trees and all the small shrubs
kneeling down like penitents.
As a child, in southern Latvia,

he used to run through the streets shouting
while the ominous clouds moved slowly
across the dark horizon
like a large foreign army
coming to liberate the village.

My grandfather used to stand calmly
by the open window during storms.
He said that he could see lightning
searching the empty rooftops,
rifling the windows for his body.

He said that rain is an ancient sign
of the sky's sadness. And he said
that he could feel the wind trying
          to lift him into its arms,
      trying to carry him home again.

Here, in the night, I'm staring
At the photograph of a stranger faking
A brave heel and toe, a lyrical
Dance with the gypsy's favorite bear
Stumbling in front of the dying
Campfire light
In a small clearing of birches
On the outskirts of Odessa. Tambourines
Flash like swords in the spoked
Shadows, and you can
Feel the drunken bear stagger
And weave with exhaustion
From too many cities, too many
Ringing triangles and suspicious eyes,
Too many bored adults, pawing children.
All the bear wants is to
Collapse in his own poor cage
Under stars scattered
Like red kerchiefs through the trees;
All he wants is to sleep. But
The stranger whispers something
Indecipherable, something convincing
In a fluent tongue, and so
The four thick arms continue to
Grip and lock and hug,
The four heavy legs stagger on.
Fur and skin. Dino Campana
And the bear. 1911. Russia.
In three long years the bear
Will have left his body forever
To travel easily, in another forest,
While the stranger will still
Be selling flowers and stoking
Furnaces, peddling songs in cafes
Out of hard need. But tonight

All he knows is that wherever
He is going is going
To be better than wherever
He is, wherever he was.
And so he tilts the bear's grim
Forehead to the sky
And keeps on dancing and dancing.
He wants to feel the moon's
Wild eye staring
Into their dark faces. He wants
To vanish into its hard, cold light.

I should have been the son of a wolf
and a bear; I should have been born
in a small cave in the forest at night;
I should have been licked clean by a mother
with thick fur and a fistful of claws,
with a roar and a howl instead of a voice.

I was named after a rampaging King of the Huns,
but Attila József isn't a name; it's a shout
from a corpse disguised as a man, it's
the twelve naked apostles of a lie, an echo
that steams in the bowels of a mirror, a proof
that ghosts wear the clothes of the living.

My father stacked crates of soap in a factory
and disappeared when I was three, a watery bucket
with a hole in it, a slippery white arm leaving
a soapy trail of blood. I was an erratic circle
rotating from a country village to a mother at home;
I was an orphaned circle searching for its center.

There's a black iron that burns in my lungs
because my mother washed laundry in an aristocrat's
house; she ironed a gentleman's white collars,
and creased his gray slacks, and steamed his jackets.
Sometimes my diminutive mother carried a skillet
of cold leftovers home for us to devour.

She slept on a rotting straw mattress on the kitchen
floor and never thought about the clouds of steam
rising from her lips, the filthy red kerchief
knotting in her chest. My mother always slept
poorly, but she was sweet and respectful and
kept a clean white apron ironed in her dreams.

I stole chickens for mama; I stole firewood
and coal from the Ferenvcáros freight yard; I
snatched red apples from the baskets at Market Hall;
I swiped bread; I waited in line for cooking lard;
I scrubbed boilers in dank basements; I sold paper
whirligigs and drinking water at the Világ Cinema.

But nothing helped. When my mother finally died
I dreamt the full moon was a tumor of the uterus,
my body was pressed under the purple iron of night.
Etus and Jolán thought we were starving suitcases
packed for a house of detention. We were so scared
that one night we sliced a ripe pear into thirds

and offered its three soft faces to the darkness
as a gift of appeasement. The darkness refused to
acknowledge the fruit, but scavengers accepted it
gladly. And yet no one—not even the crows—
can pronounce the misery of a childhood floating
through the streets at night, hanging on dark windows.

I served faithfully on the tugs Vihar, Torok, and Tatár;
I trained as a novice with the dwindling Salesian Order
at Nyergesujfalu; I taught the Bible to an idiot savant;
I guarded the huge cornfields at Kiszombor; I clerked
in a tiny bookstore and trafficked in postage stamps.
I finished the sixth year of gymnasium stifled by boredom.

My favorite colors were always blue and yellow:
the blue of self-forgetfulness, the yellow of suicide.
At nine I drank a mug of starch in the kitchen
and faked convulsions to get even with my sister.
I sobbed, howled, stamped and raged; I foamed
spectacularly at the mouth, ready to die for revenge.

At fifteen I put my right elbow on the iron tracks
and waited for the freight train to sever my arm.
But the train never lumbered through our village:
It had already killed a girl farther up the line.
Oh white owl of paranoia, I was young
and histrionic, but somebody died for me.

I was freedom's serious, dark-haired son,
a scandalous thief, a tough Hungarian punk paroled
to a life of corrections. At seventeen I begged
for radiance between hard covers, and a high court
accused me of blasphemy. Later, I was prosecuted
for claiming I had no father and no mother,

no country and no god, and I was expelled
from the university for shaking an anarchical fist
at the world in a small magazine. I was denounced,
but someone called me an infant prodigy in print,
a lyrical spokesman for the postwar generation.
No, I was just an orphan tutoring orphans.

I went to Vienna with a suitcase of bruised
manuscripts, a stick of salami, a loaf of bread
and thirty shillings. All winter I shivered
in an icy room and attended somber lectures
on the sublime in German. I sold newspapers
and scrubbed floors at the Collegium Hungaricum

until a Mæcenas sent me to the Sorbonne.
That's when I lived at 10 Rue de la Huchette
and wrote in French about the iron world of factories,
our inheritance of empty lots and slums. One night
I shouted from the rooftops that I was homesick—
I wanted the distant earth to roar in my lungs

and I missed the dark vowels of my own language.
But I was a lost European at home. In 1927
I fell in love with a wealthy girl whose parents
snatched her away from me. Oh Márta, my poppy,
I'll confess to anything but your betrayal:
indecent exposure, sedition, espionage, poverty.

I went mad twice. Once I saw the wind
kneel down in the soot like a crazed preacher;
once I saw the large red claws of darkness
scratch out the eyes of night. I hid in stairways
because I believed that the streets were on fire,
every street lamp was a warrant for my arrest.

I wanted an insurrection and in the hospital
I yelled that the rugs on the floors of all rich
merchants are the scalps of our young brothers,
the animals; I screamed that the bright roses
flowering on coffee tables in their living rooms
are the scalps of our sisters in the garden.

After that, I lived on the rim of a grave city
with an illegible scrawl on my high forehead.
My comrade and I passed out fervent red leaflets
and argued about the Paris Commune of '71, the Budapest
Commune of 1919. I joined the underground Party
but I was expelled for Trotskyist leanings.

Every winter I watched the snow gather in the streets
as the wind stripped down the stark December trees
and every year I spluttered like a village idiot
during the first hard agonies of another spring.
Every day I watched the same sun struggle out of three
smokestacks with the same smoke nestled in its arms

and every night I watched another wide moon
congealing in the clouds. I was always hungry.
One year I ate every other morning, one year
I ate every other afternoon. My darling and I
shared a double fever and slept on a narrow couch.
One night she tried to swallow a bottle of lye

and I raved against God like a blunt descendant
of Satan, or the gaunt edge of an old sickle.
Sometimes I don't know if I'm a nail or a hammer,
a handcuff or a pen, a secret or a blind omen.
I'm like a sad bear dancing in an empty forest.
I'd give my legs for a salary of two hundred pengös.

I've pawned everything but my own flesh and blood.
Today when I stood at the blank window, I discovered
a thousand wooden crosses blooming in the cemetery
and when I stared at my own reflection I realized
that my mother was a young woman when she died.
I know that I am Freud's deviant, starving son

and my button-down shoes are four sizes too big,
my pockets are filled with weightless blue pebbles.
When the Health Service sent me to a rural sanatorium
I fell in love with my analyst. I bellowed and moaned,
I invoked the faithfulness of dogs, the fatigue
of slaves, but nothing helped. And I came home.

I admit that I'm desperately in need of a job
and I'll agree to anything: I'm honest, I'm
an excellent typist, I can speak French and German,
I can take dictation and crawl on all fours.
I'm a gymnast of the dialectic and I can sing
the startled green lyrics of a prisoner's song.

This is a promissory note and a curriculum vitae,
this is a last will and testament: On April 11, 1905,
I was sentenced to thirty-two years of hard labor,
but I was innocent. Where is that freight train?
I am cutting off my right sleeve with a scissors.
I am leaving my right arm to a strange god.

Paul Celan: A Grave and Mysterious Sentence

Paris, 1948.

It's daybreak and I wish I could believe
In a rain that will wash away the morning
That is just about to rise behind the smokestacks
On the other side of the river, other side
Of nightfall. I wish I could forget the slab
Of darkness that always fails, the memories
That flood through the window in a murky light.

But now it is too late. Already the day
Is a bowl of thick smoke filling up the sky
And swallowing the river, covering the buildings
With a sickly, yellow film of sperm and milk.
Soon the streets will be awash with little bright
Patches of oblivion on their way to school,
Dark briefcases of oblivion on their way to work.

Soon my small apartment will be white and solemn
Like a blank page held up to a blank wall,
A message whispered into a vacant closet. But
This is a message which no one else remembers
Because it is stark and German, like the silence,
Like the white fire of daybreak that is burning
Inside my throat. If only I could stamp it out!

But think of smoke and ashes. An ominous string
Of railway cars scrawled with a dull pencil
Across the horizon at dawn. A girl in pigtails
Saying, "Soon you are going to be erased."
Imagine thrusting your head into a well
And crying for help in the wrong language,
Or a deaf mute shouting into an empty field.

So don't talk to me about flowers, those blind
Faces of the dead thrust up out of the ground
In bright purples and blues, oranges and reds.
And don't talk to me about the gold leaves
Which the trees are shedding like an extra skin:
They are handkerchiefs pressed over the mouths
Of the dead to keep them quiet. It's true:

Once I believed in a house asleep, a childhood
Asleep. Once I believed in a mother dreaming
About a pair of giant iron wings growing
Painfully out of the shoulders of the roof
And lifting us into away-from-here-and-beyond.
Once I even believed in a father calling out
In the dark, restless and untransfigured.

But what did we know then about the smoke
That was already beginning to pulse from trains,
To char our foreheads, to transform their bodies
Into two ghosts billowing from a huge oven?
What did we know about a single gray strand
Of barbed wire knotted slowly and tightly
Around their necks? We didn't know anything then.

And now here is a grave and mysterious sentence
Finally written down, carried out long ago:
At last I have discovered that the darkness
Is a solitary night train carrying my parents
Across a field of dead stumps and wildflowers
Before disappearing on the far horizon,
Leaving nothing much in its earthly wake

But a stranger standing at the window
Suddenly trying to forget his childhood,
To forget a black trail of smoke
Slowly unraveling in the distance
Like the victory-flag of death, to forget
The slate clarity of another day
Forever breaking behind the smokestacks.

In a Polish Home
for the Aged (Chicago, 1983)

It's sweet to lie awake in the early morning
Remembering the sound of five huge bells
Ringing in the village at dawn, the iron
Notes turning to music in the pink clouds.

It's nice to remember the flavor of groats
Mixed with horse's blood, the sour tang
Of unripe peppers, the smell of garlic
Growing in Aunt Stefania's garden.

I can remember my grandmother's odd claim
That her younger brother was a mule
Pulling an ox cart across a lapsed meadow
In the first thin light of a summer morning;

Her cousin, Irka, was a poorly planted tree
Wrapping itself in a dress of white blossoms.
I could imagine an ox cart covered with flowers,
The sound of laughter coming from damp branches.

Some nights I dream that I'm a child again
Flying through the barnyard at six a.m.:
My mother milks the cows in the warm barn
And thinks about her father, who died long ago,

And daydreams about my future in a large city.
I want to throw my arms around her neck
And touch the sweating blue pails of milk
And talk about my childish nightmares.

God, you've got to see us to know how happy
We were then, two dark caresses of sunlight.
Now I wake up to the same four walls staring
At me blankly, and the same bare ceiling.

The morning starts over in the home:
Someone coughs in the hall, someone calls out
An unfamiliar name, a name I don't remember,
Someone slams a car door in the distance.

I touch my feet to the cold tile floor
And listen to my neighbor stirring in his room
And think about my mother's peculiar words
After my grandmother died during the war:

"One day the light will be as thick as a pail
Of fresh milk, but the pail will seem heavy.
You won't know if you can lift it anymore,
But lift it anyway. Drink the day slowly."

1

For some of us it began with wild dogs
Howling like dirges in the early morning
And crazed wolves answering in the distance.

It began with the shrieking of peacocks
And three mad sables roving through the streets
And a sound of donkeys screeching like children.

Some of us heard the polar bears wailing
And two African giraffes whining in terror
At the death throes of a baby elephant

And we knew it had begun in earnest.
But some people refuse to imagine zebras
Careening around in hysterical circles,

Or cheetahs smashing their cages, or bats
Clinging to crippled leopards and then
Floating over their heads in a broad light.

Some people need to see the sky speaking
German, and the night wearing a steel helmet,
And the moon slowly turning into a swastika.

2

But then we saw the stomach of the city
Burning in the distance, all the charred
Sugar and fresh meats, all the white flour

And dark grains flaming on the far horizon
In oily black clouds of smoke tinged
With ember-reds and soiled brown mauves.

It was like seeing hundreds of waves of
Blood rolling over the city at dusk and then
Hanging in heavy layers under the stars.

No one cried out or screamed in pain
To see our crumbling wooden depots of food
Climbing in swollen clouds into the sky

But a few children who were already hungry
And an old man who saw his own small intestine
Drifting like a balloon over his wife's head.

That's how in Peter the Great's white showcase
Built on a vast swamp on the northernmost
Fringe of Europe, we began to starve.

3

It's to lie in the dark at four a.m.
Thinking about the sweetness of surrender,
What the mind yields to a mattress in fatigue

And the body forgets to remember, what
The reluctant night yields to a cold room
Where windows are boarded with plywood

And light searches for a crack in the roof.
It's to remember the women with bright parasols
Strolling down the wide Parisian boulevards

And the men cruising in black limousines.
It's to forget the words "typhoid" and "cholera,"
The sirens that go on wailing in your sleep.

There are days when dying will seem as
Easy as sitting down in a warm, comfortable
Overstuffed chair and going back to sleep,

Or lying in bed for hours. But you must
Not sit down, you must spend your life digging
Out trenches with a shovel, staying awake.

4

So whoever will eat must work and whoever
Will survive must fight. But the sick
Civilians shiver on narrow gray stretchers

In the dark in unheated hospital rooms,
The soldiers respect the terror of their wounds.
There is no water, no warmth, and no light

And the bodies keep piling up in the corridor.
A red soldier tears his mouth from a bandage
And announces to a young nurse, "Darling,

Tanks are what we need now, beautiful tanks,
Beloved tanks rolling over the barren fields
And playing their music in the pink sky."

No one pays attention, but a volunteer regrets
That trolleys have stopped running to the front:
He'll have to walk the distance. Meanwhile,

The bodies keep piling up in the corridor
And a dazed girl keeps shouting, "But I *can*
Fight the Nazis!" Whoever can fight will eat.

5

I have lanced the boils on every finger
And sucked the warm pus; I have eaten
A thin jelly made of leather straps,

And swallowed the acrid green oil cakes,
And tasted a cold extract of pine needles.
I have stared at the flayed white trees

And watched my children chasing a scrawny
Cat through the streets at dawn, and smelled
The dead cat boiling in my own kitchen.

I have tried to relinquish judgment,
To eat the cat or the dog without disgust.
I have seen starved women begging for rations

And starved men crawling under a frozen black
Sun, and I have turned my back slowly.
I have waited in a thousand lines for bread,

But I won't gouge at another human body;
I won't eat the sweet breasts of a murdered
Woman, or the hacked thighs of a dying man.

6

After we burned the furniture and the books
In the stove, we were always cold, always:
But we got used to icicles in our chests.

We got used to the fires falling from the sky
At dusk, spreading across the scorched roofs.
And we got used to the formula of edible

Cellulose and cottonseed cakes and dry meal dust
And a pinch of corn flour for our dark bread.
We got used to our own stomachs bulging with air.

And then one day the bodies started to appear
Piled on the bright sleds of little children,
Bundled up in thick curtains and torn sheets

And old rags and sometimes even in newspapers.
We saw the staircases jammed with corpses,
The doorways and the dead-end alleys, and smelled

A scent of turpentine hanging in the frosty air.
We got used to leaving our dead unburied,
Stacked like cordwood in the drifts of snow.

7

Somehow we lived with our empty stomachs
And our ankles in chains, somehow we managed
With a heavy iron collar wrapped tightly

Around our necks. Sometimes the sun seemed
Like a German bomber, or an air-raid warden,
Or a common foot soldier speaking German.

We saw houses that had been sliced in two
From the attic to the cellar and large buildings
That had been blown apart like small windows.

We saw a soldier cradling a kneecap in his palms
And children watching the soft red fluids
Of their intestines flowing through their fingers.

We saw a girl tearing out clumps of hair
And surgeons who tried to scratch out their eyes
Because they couldn't stand to see their hands.

Slowly we touched a sharp razor to our necks
And scraped away the useless blue skin
And the dead flesh. Somehow we lived.

4

It was as if the rain could feel itself
falling through the air today, as if the air
could actually feel its own dampness, the breeze
could hear a familiar voice explaining the emptiness
to the dark elms that swayed unconsciously along
the wet road, the elms that could still feel
their own branches glistening with rain.

It was as if the sky had imagined a morning
of indigos and pinks, mauves and reddish-browns.
The smiling young nurse who helped you into the car
was wearing two colorful ribbons in her auburn hair and
somehow they looked precisely like ribbons gleaming
in the hair of a woman helping you into a car.
I believe I had never seen ribbons before.

And suddenly I was staring at asphalt
puddled with rainwater. And bluish letters
purpling on a white sign. And sliding electric
ENTRANCES & EXITS. And statues bristling with color.
The yellow sunlight filtered through the clouds
and I believe I had never seen a street lamp
shimmer across a wavy puddle before.

The road home was slick with lights
and everything seemed to be crying, *just
this, just this, nothing more, nothing else!*—
as if the morning were somehow conscious of itself.
When you leaned over and touched me on the arm
it was as if my arm needed to be touched
in that way, at exactly that time.

Whoever has followed the bag lady
on her terrible journey past Food Lane's Super-Market,
and Maze's Records, and The Little Flowering Barbershop
on the southeast corner of Woodward and Euclid
will know what it meant for John Clare
to walk eighty miles across pocked and jutted
roads to Northborough, hungry, shy of strangers,
"foot foundered and broken down" after escaping
from the High Beech Asylum near Epping Forest.
And whoever has followed the bag lady
on her studious round of littered stairwells
and dead-end alleys, and watched her combing
the blue and white city garbage cans for empties,
and admired the way that she can always pick out
the single plate earring and one Canadian dime
from a million splinters of glass in a phone booth
will know how John Clare must have looked
as he tried to follow the route that a gypsy
had pointed out for him, scaling the high
palings that stood in his way, bruising
his feet on the small stones, stooping to
admire the pileworts and cowslips, scorning
the self-centered cuckoos but knowing the sweet
kinship of a landrail hiding in the hedgerows.

I began this morning by standing
in front of the New World Church's ruined storefront;
I was listening to the bag lady and a pimply-
faced old drunk trading secrets with the vent man,
and remembering how a gentleman on horseback
had mistaken John Clare for a broken-down haymaker
and tossed him a penny for a half-pint of beer.
I remembered how grateful he was to stand
elbow to elbow in the Old Plough Public House
happily sheltered from a sudden rainfall.

But later when I saw the bag lady
sprawled out on a steaming vent for warmth
I remembered how Clare had moved on, crippled
by tiny bits of gravel lodged in his shoes,
and how he tried to escape from the harsh wind
by lying down in an open dike bottom
but was soaked through clear to his bones;
how he came to the heavy wooden doors
of the Wild Ram Public House hours later,
and gazed longingly at the brightly lit windows,
and had no money, and passed on. Whoever
has stood alone in the night's deep shadows
listening to laughter coming from a well-lit house
will know that John Clare's loneliness was unbending.
And whoever has felt that same unbending loneliness
will also know what an old woman felt today
as she followed an obedient path between the huge
green garbage cans behind Kroger's Super-Market
and the small silver ones behind Clarence's grocery.

I began this day by following a bag lady
in honor of John Clare but suddenly, tonight,
I was reading "The Journey Out of Essex, 1841,"
in honor of the unknown bag lady.
I had witnessed a single day in her life
and was trying hard not to judge myself
and judging myself anyway.
I remember how she stooped to rub her foot;
how she smiled a small toothful grin
when she discovered a half-eaten apple;
how she talked on endlessly to herself
and fell asleep leaning against a broken wall
in an abandoned wooden shed on Second Avenue.
Tonight when I lie down in the dark
in my own bed, I want to remember

that John Clare was so desperately hungry
after three days and nights without food
that he finally knelt down, as if in prayer,
and ate the soft grass of the earth,
and thought it tasted like fresh bread,
and judged no one, not even himself,
and slept peacefully again, like a child.

Excuses

If only I could begin to sift through the smoke
rising from the wet streets leading to your small room

above the warehouse. If only I didn't have to walk
to one side of myself, sideways, like a shadow

growing out of the side of a building, painfully.
If only the yellow light across the street

wasn't so ashamed
of the three iron stairs and the empty doorway

that no one crosses in the sullen rainfall,
or afterwards. It's the way the wind rearranges

the puddles after a storm, the trees hang
upside down in the water, and no starlings call.

Or it's the way the past revises itself
in my mind, searching for a white stone

to mark the place, to find my way back
to the small room that is no longer

your room
above a warehouse that is no longer a warehouse

but the memory of an enormous wooden space
hollowed out of the night. If only I could

find us sleeping there, suspended
over the unrevised space, tangled or spoonlike,

then I wouldn't have to spend this night
walking to one side of myself,

standing beside myself,
paralyzed by the memory of you

in the middle of a vacant city block.
If only I could stop standing here, sideways,

like a shadow growing out of the fleshy side
of an abandoned building, painfully,

like a shadow on fire.

Unhappy Love Poem

I wanted to lie. I wanted to say
   it was the rain falling through a fine mist
      and shattering the lake into tiny fragments

that suddenly brought it home to me today
   in warm shocks, in a blazing purple gust
      as I walked by the water in the early morning.

I wanted to invent the wildest statements
   about what happened to us, to feel brilliant
      and wronged, like an angry young widow mowing

the front yard in a strapless evening gown,
   or a born-again Christian suddenly jumping
      into a fountain to wash away his sins.

I never wanted it to be like this: hopeless
   and ordinary, dull as a toothache at lunchtime,
      as watching t.v. in the afternoon in summer.

I never wanted it to happen inside the house
   where I am still undressed at 2 p.m., at 4 p.m.,
      where it seems so precisely like failure.

The White Blackbird

"Imagine for a moment that the white blackbird
has gone blind. . . ."   —JEAN-PAUL SARTRE

The morning after Sartre's death

I thought of a hundred blackbirds rising
Out of a brilliant white lake sheeted with mist,
Covering the sky with their feathery bodies

And blotting the sun with their dark cries.

I was sitting alone on the twisted wooden
Stairs of a rented house in the country,
Reading about Sartre's long blindness

And watching the crows in a neighbor's yard

Descending on the body of a twisted sycamore.
Those birds were a mistake, a dozen black
Errors scrawled across an empty page

In the sudden stark blankness of morning.

It was for Sartre that I remembered a blaze
Of dark scavengers emerging out of a cold lake
In the torturous outer calm of springtime.

And it was for Sartre

That I remembered a single white blackbird
Drifting over the metallic water at noon, lost
And severed from the other birds, blinded

By the clarity and madness of sunlight.

Like a stunned piano, like a bucket
of fresh milk flung into the air
or a dozen fists of confetti
thrown hard at a bride
stepping down from the altar,
the stars surprise the sky.
Think of dazed stones
floating overhead, or an ocean
of starfish hung up to dry. Yes,
like a conductor's expectant arm
about to lift toward the chorus,
or a juggler's plates defying gravity,
or a hundred fastballs fired at once
and freezing in midair, the stars
startle the sky over the city.

And that's why drunks leaning up
against abandoned buildings, women
hurrying home on deserted side streets,
policemen turning blind corners, and
even thieves stepping from alleys
all stare up at once. Why else do
sleepwalkers move toward the windows,
or old men drag flimsy lawn chairs
onto fire escapes, or hardened criminals
press sad foreheads to steel bars?
Because the night is alive with lamps!
That's why in dark houses all over the city
dreams stir in the pillows, a million
plumes of breath rise into the sky.

A Dark Hillside

Out here in the last moments before dusk,
It is strange to see the way that shadows
Steep in the tall grass and sunlight falls,
Like a woman's naked arm, across the porch
And the dim shoulders of the house.

And it is strange to be standing *here*
Instead of *there*, with my hands darkening
Inside my pockets, staring for so long
At a single blue fir spiraling
Out of the forehead of a nearby hill

That it begins to resemble the golden
Horn of a mythical beast, a stray animal
That men have been seeking for centuries.
Every child knows what a unicorn is
Though no one has ever seen anything

But a tapestry, or a well-executed
Illustration, or a faulty copy of one;
And yet this never seemed mysterious
To me before now, until today. I don't
Know if it is curious or not

To seek the trembling blues and yellows
Of dusk as often as I have, or to feel
Strangeness seeping through the air
Until nothing seems like what it is,
Nothing is what it seems. I don't know

If children believe in tapestries anymore,
Or in cobblestone streets in old engravings,
Or in blue horses moving across the sky. . . .
But sometimes when I drift through
The afternoon's deep shadows, the silence

Of the country at dusk can still
Seem like a kind of promise, a pact
Between the red elms and the dusky clouds
Reaching down to engulf them—and somehow,
The hills can still take on the dreamy,

Faraway look of a man standing at the window
High in the crown of his house,
Knowing that no one—not his wife
Descending the stairs, not his children
Running through the yard—can see him.

Standing there at the level of the trees
He could believe in the stars again,
Slowly being released into the sky,
One by one, like long yellow plumes
Of breath, calm and precise above us;

He could believe in the light again
Flying toward him through the clouds. . . .
I have no idea who he is,
Or why he is here now, alone
In my mind's eye, absent-mindedly

Staring at a purple blend of shadows
Weaving through the long hair of the elms.
And suddenly I have no idea why
I am telling all of this to *you*,
You who are so unknown to me,

As if there could be something like
Intimacy between us, as if I could ever
Communicate anything so mysterious,
Anything so austere and familiar
As even this simple story, written down:

Once, in the slow shadings of dusk,
In the middle of his life,
A man moved toward a blue unicorn.
He was a stranger
Crossing a deserted road, alone.

He was a late-afternoon shadow
Lengthening across the tall grass,
Darkening on a dark hillside.

Soon we will give our speechless bodies
Back to the garden at night, like the scores
Of old songs we can no longer quite remember,
Or the embroidered shirts we outgrew as children.
Once, their colorful new skins clung tightly
To our skins, molding to our elastic human
Shapes, but now they hang limply in thrift shops
Next to coverless issues of *Newsweek* and *Time*
And sullen piano music that no longer wants
To remember the slow torture of being played
On endless rainy afternoons in mid-October.
Sometimes I think that inside one of those faded
Musical sheets I am still practicing scales,
Still trying to avoid the musty gray smell
Of an interminable Sunday at home (and sometimes
I think the dullest afternoons of adulthood are
A memory of childhood relived in a tedium of autumn).

I used to press my forehead against the window
And imagine the sun moving behind the buildings
Like an exhausted old woman tramping home
Through a field after a long day in the city
With her hands buried deep in the pockets
Of a flowering red dress. I liked to pretend
That she would leave a smoky lantern flaming
In the elms for luck while she hummed a lullaby
To herself, a song from some other world,
The secret of light. I'd strain to listen,
But all I could hear was the voicelessness
Of the wind blowing its emptiness across the sad
Rooftops, leafing through the empty pages of trees.
All I could see was my own childish, blue boredom.
I am thirty-five now, but sometimes when I look out
At the garden at dusk, I can still feel myself
Becoming that child again, reliving that boredom,

And suddenly I am afraid only that the garden is
Changing even as we are changing, even as the sun
Goes back to being a sun toiling behind purple bars
On the horizon, and our bodies start to wear out
Like our favorite suits and hats. It's the way
That even the fat crabapple tree swelling up
By the fence will someday retire from giving fruit
To every poor scavenger that comes along, every
Obese squirrel and thin starling, every lost crow.
Soon the sour green tree will quit storing up
Food for the moles—soon, but not yet.
Because look how the garden survives the dusk,
How quietly it waits for us, how lovingly
It welcomes us back. Maybe it already knows
That we always return to its soil like husbands
Who never quite leave their faithless wives,
Or sons who grow into their own fathers.

So, too, we will touch our bodies to the soil
And know the ground by its damp and bitter taste.
But until then, I will stand by the window at dusk
Remembering the sullen blue notes of a forgotten
Childhood, the tedious hours practicing, the rainy
Afternoons that seem eternal in an adult's memory.
I will remember a slow dream of leaving the house
And then walk through the garden on cool nights
Listening for a single redbreasted cardinal
That sometimes returns to our dark elms. I
Like to think it is a little explosion of dye
Erupting in secret in its own time, a minor
Echo of the sun toiling on the bruised horizon.
I like to believe it is a smoky red lantern
That an old woman leaves in the branches
To fend off the darkness while she sleeps,
To keep a red flame burning through the night.

Some nights when you're asleep
Deep under the covers, far away,
Slowly curling yourself back
Into a childhood no one
Living will ever remember
Now that your parents touch hands
Under the ground
As they always did upstairs
In the master bedroom, only more
Distant now, deaf to the nightmares,
The small cries that no longer
Startle you awake but still
Terrify me so that
I do get up, some nights, restless
And anxious to walk through
The first trembling blue light
Of dawn in a calm snowfall.
It's soothing to see the houses
Asleep in their own large bodies,
The dreamless fences, the courtyards
Unscarred by human footprints,
The huge clock folding its hands
In the forehead of the skyscraper
Looming downtown. In the park
The benches are layered in
White, the statue out of history
Is an outline of blue snow. Cars,
Too, are rimmed and motionless
Under a thin blanket smoothed down
By the smooth maternal palm
Of the wind. So thanks to the
Blue morning, to the blue spirit
Of winter, to the soothing blue gift
Of powdered snow! And soon
A few scattered lights come on

In the houses, a motor coughs
And starts up in the distance, smoke
Raises its arms over the chimneys.
Soon the trees suck in the darkness
And breathe out the light
While black drapes open in silence.
And as I turn home where
I know you are already awake,
Wandering slowly through the house
Searching for me, I can suddenly
Hear my own footsteps crunching
The simple astonishing news
That we are here,
Yes, we are still here.

ACKNOWLEDGMENTS

Grateful acknowledgment is made to the editors of the following publications where these poems—many of which have been substantially revised—first appeared:

Antaeus: "Indian Summer," "Recovery"
The Antioch Review: "Three Journeys"
The Atlantic: "Fast Break"
Crazyhorse: "The Village Idiot," "Paul Celan: A Grave and Mysterious Sentence," "The Emaciated Horse"
Fiction International: "Excuses," "Unhappy Love Poem"
The Georgia Review: "The Night Parade"
Grand Street: "In a Polish Home for the Aged (Chicago, 1983)"
Kayak: "Sleepwatch"
Memphis State Review: "The Secret"
Michigan Quarterly Review: "Leningrad (1941–1943)"
The Missouri Review: "Omen," "The Skokie Theatre"
The Nation: "In the Middle of August," "Dino Campana and the Bear" copyright © 1981, 1982 The Nation Associates, Inc.
National Forum: "Prelude of Black Drapes," "In Spite of Everything, the Stars"
The New Republic: "Wild Gratitude"
The New Yorker: "I Need Help," "Fall," "Dawn Walk"
The Ontario Review: "Curriculum Vitae (1937)"
Ploughshares: "Commuters"
Poetry: "Edward Hopper and the House by the Railroad (1925)," "A Dark Hillside" (under the title "Moving Toward a Blue Unicorn"), "Fever," "Poor Angels"
Shenandoah: "The White Blackbird"
Skywriting: "Ancient Signs" (under the title "My Grandfather Loved Storms")

The epigraph is from W. H. Auden, *Selected Poems*: New Edition (New York: Vintage, 1979), p. 89.

I wish to express my gratitude to the National Endowment for the Arts and to Wayne State University for their support during the writing of this book. "Dawn Walk" is in memory of Gertrude Landay (1916–1979) and Donald Landay (1914–1977). "The Night Parade" is dedicated to Susan Stewart. "Curriculum Vitae (1937)" is for Lawrence Joseph.

Special thanks to Alice Quinn for her encouragement and generosity.

A NOTE ON THE TYPE

This book was set on the Linotype in Granjon, a type named in compliment to Robert Granjon, type cutter and printer in Antwerp, Lyons, Rome, Paris. Granjon, the boldest and most original designer of his time, was one of the first to practice the trade of type founder apart from that of printer.

Linotype Granjon was designed by George W. Jones, who based his drawings on a face used by Claude Garamond (1510–1561) in his beautiful French books. Granjon more closely resembles Garamond's own type than do any of the various modern faces that bear his name.

Composed by Maryland Linotype Composition Company, Baltimore, Maryland
Printed and bound by Halliday Lithographers, Inc., West Hanover, Massachusetts
Designed by Iris Weinstein